Divorce Is Not the End of the World:

Zoe's and Evan's Coping Guide for Kids

ZOE AND **EVAN STERN**

With a little help from their mom,
ELLEN SUE STERN

TRICYCLE PRESS
Berkeley, California

To my incredibly amazing mama, for always standing with me in times of trouble and for being so very cool. You are my soul mate.
—Zoe

This book is dedicated to my sister, Zoe.
—Evan

For my incredible children, Zoe and Evan, for being the sweetest blessing in my life. I love you forever.
—Mom

TRICYCLE PRESS
P.O. Box 7123
Berkeley, California 94707

Book Design by Toni Tajima
Cover illustration © 1997 Kyrsten Brooker

Library of Congress Cataloging-in-Publication Data
Stern, Zoe.
    Divorce is not the end of the world/Zoe's and Evan's coping guide for kids/Zoe Stern and Evan Stern with a little help from their mom, Ellen Sue Stern.
        p.   cm.
    Summary: A teenage brother and sister whose parents are divorced discuss topics relating to this situation, respond to letters from other children, and offer tips based on their experience. Includes insights from their mother.
    ISBN 1-883672-44-9
    1. Children of divorced parents—Juvenile literature. 2. Divorced parents—Juvenile literature. 3. Divorce—Juvenile literature. 4. Remarriage—Juvenile literature. 5. Stepfamilies—Juvenile literature. [1. Divorce. 2. Remarriage 3. Stepfamilies.] I. Stern, Evan. II. Stern, Ellen Sue, 1954-. III. Title.
HQ777.5.S73 1997   97-624
306.89—dc21   CIP
                                                                     AC

First Tricycle Press Printing, 1997
Manufactured in Singapore
        3 4 5 6 — 01 00 99 98

Contents

ACKNOWLEDGMENTS . . . .

ZOE'S ACKNOWLEDGMENTS: I wish to thank Lyndsay Obbarius, Claire Seiwert, Amy Arguedas, Lilly Benson, Jessie Lewis, and Sarah Steiger for always being there. You are "the girls." Lindsay Rosen, for telling me there's never a dumb question. Natalie Fursetzer, for being my role model. Amy Silver, for reminding me of who I am. Sam Gordon, Betsey Krause, and Sara Gordon, for listening to my stories. Mollie Moore-Goldstein and Rae Solomon for teaching me how to fly. And my dad, for always being patient.

EVAN'S ACKNOWLEDGMENTS: I want to thank Mom for creating this book and always finding something for me to eat. To my friends, Nate Uri and Noah Freed, for helping me occupy my time. And thanks to Dad and Demetrios for making me laugh.

ELLEN SUE'S ACKNOWLEDGMENTS: A debt of gratitude goes to Nicole Geiger, whose fine editing, sensitivity, and humor greatly enhanced this book. To David Hinds, for believing in this project and being a constant "ear." To Mollie Moore-Goldstein, Rae Solomon, Martina Barbour-Pustinsky, Liliana Barbour-Pustinsky, and all the other courageous and resilient kids who continue to inspire my belief that kids of divorce are truly heroic.

ZOE'S INTRODUCTION . . . . . .

THE REASON I'M WRITING THIS BOOK is because I've been through divorce and will always be a "divorced kid." I know that it's really hard and it hurts. I hope this book will help any and all kids who are hurting or in need of some comforting and advice. Hopefully, the "Dear Zoe" portion of this book will help answer some of the many questions I've been asked by kids who are going through the same thing. For me, my parents' divorce was hard at first, but I overcame my sadness and my fears about it. I know that my parents are happier apart. And I'm happy with the way things are, too. I hope that, through this book, you will realize that divorce can sometimes be for the better. You may end up with happier parents, and you will definitely learn a lot about yourself! And that's the whole point of growing up. So if you think about it, there are reasons to be happy about this experience, if you can learn and grow from it.

EVAN'S INTRODUCTION . . . . .

IT'S OBVIOUS THAT DIVORCE IS HARD—you have to let it sink in and cry and talk to your parents. It may not feel good, like a shot doesn't feel good but does your body good. Divorce does your soul good because it's a hard emotional experience that makes you stronger. It's like taking a quiz: A test checks out how you are, but a quiz prepares you for the test of life. I don't think kids have all these problems parents think they do. Grown-ups are worried that they're going to ruin their children's lives, but divorce is just a life experience and you learn from it. I'm a different person because of it, and you will be too. If nothing else, you'll have learned that there are at least two other kids who've been through this so you know you're not alone.

ELLEN SUE'S INTRODUCTION . . .

LIKE EVERY PARENT I KNOW, my decision to divorce was an agonizing, heartwrenching process that involved a great deal of soul-searching. I knew that my marriage had to end, but I could hardly bear the thought of putting my children through such a traumatic experience. I was racked with fear, guilt, and anxiety. How would Evan and Zoe, then six and eight years old, survive? How would we handle their birthday parties? Bar and bat mitzvahs? High school graduations? Would they be forever wounded by coming from a "broken home"? Would they end up spending 20 years in therapy? All my hopes and dreams of us having the "perfect family" were slowly shattered as I faced what I was about to do.

When Evan was three years old, sitting in his car seat on our way home from nursery school, he said something I've never forgotten. In all the innocence of childhood, he told me, "I know you and Daddy will never get divorced." "Why not?" I asked. "Because you love me and Zoey too much," he replied. These words echoed as their father and I sat down to tell our kids the news: "Daddy and I love you very much, but we've decided we need to live apart." I watched in horror as they recoiled in disbelief, then ran from the room, sobbing. Some 20 minutes later, they reappeared in the living room, holding hands, wanting to know: "If you and Daddy get divorced, will we have two VCRs—one at each house?" At that moment, I knew they'd be okay.

Better than okay. Today I can say with pride and confidence that my children have turned out to be incredibly strong, brave, resilient, and compassionate human beings, in part because of what they have been through. Witnessing how Zoe and Evan have survived and thrived has made me question the widely believed idea that children of divorce are at risk for dangerous and self-destructive behavior and may be less capable of creating successful, long-term intimate relationships. On the contrary, as is evident throughout this book, kids who have been through divorce are often stronger, more flexible, and capable of handling change.

Working with Zoe and Evan on this book reinforced this belief and gave me some suprising insights into how differently their generation sees divorce. When I was growing up, I knew a few kids whose parents were divorced; we spoke of them in hushed tones, seeing them as outcasts deserving of sympathy. Yet Zoe and Evan altered my perceptions, especially when I asked them questions such as: "Do you wish you came from a 'normal' family?" and "Do you worry about whether there's any such thing as a happy marriage?" to which they replied by looking at me as if I was nuts. These thoughts had never occurred to them, in large part because they don't consider themselves abnormal or a minority, since over half their friends' parents are divorced.

No parent would wish to ever have to say to their children: "Daddy (or Mommy) and I are getting a divorce." Yet those of us who must do so can do a great deal to help our children transform this into a positive experience. In working therapeutically with individuals and families, I have come to realize that it is not the painful experiences of our lives that wound us, but rather how they are—or in most cases, aren't—dealt with that create lasting scars. To help our kids survive and thrive from the experience of divorce, we must first and foremost respect their real feelings. No matter how much we wish we could do so, we cannot "make it better" by telling them that everything will be okay. We need to accept that we cannot make their pain disappear, but rather we must make a safe space in which they can freely express their emotions. We can offer support, we can love them with all our hearts, but ultimately, they must go through this transition in their own way, in their own time.

It's been said that "life works in mysterious ways." I truly believe that both my marriage and my divorce were meant to be, and that I and my children are better as a result of what we have been through. We have written this book in the hope that other kids and parents will find wisdom and comfort as they find their way through this life-changing experience.

Why Did This Have to Happen?

WHEN YOUR PARENTS GET DIVORCED

Evan: Of course I wondered, "Why did this have to happen to me?" But some things in life just happen. Why do airplanes crash? Why do some people get cancer? Why did Celtic Stadium get torn down? Why do I need glasses and my sister doesn't?

Zoe: At first, you look for reasons. It's just too weird to imagine your parents not being together. In my case, even though I was just eight and my brother was six, my parents told us the truth...that they were getting divorced because my father was gay. So at least there was a good reason. But I still had lots of questions, like wanting to know if my mom had known and if so, why did she marry him? And if he knew, how could he have caused such a big problem?

Evan: I see what you mean, but if you think about it, *Why?* is kind of a rhetorical question. There's no good answer, except that God does things for different purposes. You may not know the reasons at the time, and of course, it feels bad, but feeling bad is fine—it's part of it. You have to let yourself feel the bad stuff in order to experience the good stuff.

Zoe: That's true. As time goes on, you get used to it and stop feeling so bad. But you also may have more questions that pop up. There was a period of time when I saw my father spending a lot of time with a close woman friend, and I got really upset and wondered if he'd changed his mind, in which case I'd have been really, really mad. For a long time, I thought my parents would have stayed together if my dad wasn't gay. But now that I'm older, I see that things are more complicated and I think they might have split up anyway.

Evan: Maybe, maybe not. You can keep trying to figure out what could have happened differently or you can accept that what happened was exactly what was supposed to happen. Of course, if you turn it upside down, you realize that good things happen too, without any explanation. Hopefully, the good and the bad balance out.

Zoe: In our family, I really think this has turned out to be true. Over time, I've realized that my parents are happier and better people than they were before. I can see why the divorce was necessary for them to each live their own lives. They've been through the worst and there was no way to go but up, so that's the way they went.

Evan: Bad experiences often turn into good experiences even if you can't see it at the time. That bumper sticker saying "Stuff Happens" is true, and you just have to accept that there may not be any good answer, except "that's life."

Dear Zoe,

I thought everything was great in our family and then boom! Everything fell apart. My parents fought over stuff, but I had no idea things were this serious. It would have really helped if they would have at least told me that they were considering a divorce. I don't understand why if my parents loved each other once, they can't just work out their problems instead of breaking up our family. Don't you think adults should be more responsible and mature?

Helen, age 13

Dear Helen,

You sound angry and I don't blame you a bit. It would be a huge shock to think everything's pretty much okay and then just get told that your parents have made this huge decision that affects you as much as them. Even though I think you're old enough that you should have been given more information, your parents may have wanted to protect you and not say anything until they were absolutely sure. Obviously, their plan backfired. As far as why this had to happen, it's really hard to accept that grown-ups can't always make things work. Even if your parents still love each other, they may not be able to live together anymore. They may have tried really hard, going to marriage counseling and everything, and have just come to the end of their rope. You should ask your parents to explain their reasons—it's never too late—but it still may be hard to understand all the ins and outs. Being a kid, you just have to trust that your parents thought this all out very carefully and that this is the only solution that will work.

Good luck,
Zoe

──────── Evan's Quick Tips ────────

1. Ask why. You may or may not get a good answer, but it's worth a try.

2. Go ahead and feel sorry for yourself for a while. Eventually, you'll get sick of it and go on with your life.

3. Give yourself lots of time to understand what has happened.

4. Think about all the times your parents fought or seemed unhappy. That might help you realize that the divorce may be for the best.

5. Give in to the mysteries of life.

What Their Mom Has to Say _____

All kids want to know why their parents are getting divorced. They better have a really good reason for putting you through this, right? When Zoe and Evan asked why we were getting divorced, their father and I felt it was important to tell them the truth, even if it hurt. But it isn't so easy for parents to explain how and why they've come to the point where it's necessary to part. They want you to understand their reasons in a way that will make sense to you, but they don't want you to worry about their personal problems. That's why they might not give you enough information, or they might say things that don't really help, like "You'll understand when you're older." You have the right to ask why, and you should keep asking as many times as you need.

You might also think of some of the reasons *you* believe your parents needed to get divorced. For example, maybe they argued a lot. Maybe they couldn't work out their differences, even though they tried very hard. Or maybe they simply grew apart.

If you need more information, ask. But even if you get a "good answer," it may still take time for you to accept what's happening. As Evan says, "There may not be any good reason, except 'that's life.'" What he means is hang in there and in time the reasons will become clearer.

Your Turn _____

Have you asked your parents to tell you why they're getting divorced?

Are you satisfied with their answer?

Can you think of some reasons why it was necessary for your parents to get divorced?

. . . .

IT MAY TAKE A LONG TIME
FOR ME TO UNDERSTAND AND
ACCEPT WHY THIS HAD TO
HAPPEN.

. . . .

Maybe They'll Get Back Together 2

HOPES, SCHEMES, AND SECRET FANTASIES

Zoe: Lots of times the very first thing you think is, "Will they get back together?" I mean, maybe they're just going through a rough patch and can iron things out. But then you ask them and they say "No," so you get it that it's pretty serious and you might as well be realistic. Kids think it may be possible that their parents will reunite because it's what they're used to; they've spent their whole lives seeing their parents as a unit and knowing they have lots of feelings for each other. So if they knew how to be together all this time, maybe they can figure out how to get the feelings back.

Evan: I remember having some of these fantasies. Thoughts like this don't always happen at the beginning, right when your parents say they're getting divorced. Usually these fantasies are very brief and may occur to you when one of your parents moves out and it starts to get real. You'll be doing something normal and you'll think about your parents getting together. You get hopeful, but it's kind of depressing because deep down you know it won't happen. You envision it and you get excited. I suppose it's possible that they may change their minds, but I wouldn't count on it because then you might get disappointed.

Zoe: I agree. It doesn't help to fantasize because you need to move on and you can't move on if you keep wishing it would change. I knew my parents weren't gonna get back together because my Dad had made his choice to spend his time with a man instead of a woman. I felt as if that was a very final decision. There are other circumstances where it might not seem so final, but usually it is. You have to accept reality, but you might not be able to do that—until you've convinced yourself that there's no way to change it and that you may as well shake off the fantasies and get real.

Evan: But there's also a good reason for having fantasies. I was starting a new school and when I got really sad about losing all my old friends, my dad explained that there are five stages of grief. They are shock, denial, anger, bargaining, and acceptance. Secret fantasies of your parents getting back together is the bargaining part, when you start thinking of ways to change it because you just can't accept that it's really true. Fantasizing is something you have to do in order to realize the truth. It's like when you turn in a school project and you know it's pretty bad and you fantasize about getting a good grade. It's a way of preparing yourself to deal with only getting a C. If you play out your fantasies, you eventually realize they're all in your head and aren't going to happen, at which point you can get down to living with reality.

Dear Zoe,

My parents recently got divorced and I have a great plan on how to get them back together. Here it is: I'm going to tell my mom to meet me for dinner at my favorite Vietnamese restaurant. Then I'll tell my dad to also meet me there. Just as we all sit down to eat, I'll disappear to the bathroom with a stomachache. They'll be worried so they'll both come back to Mom's house to take care of me. I'll fall asleep and they'll sit on the couch and one thing will lead to another. I think this may work since they both love me and will realize what a terrible mistake they've made.

Avram, age 11

Dear Avram,

That was a really creative plan and you seem like a really creative guy, but maybe you should use that creativity in another way. Your parents probably will not get back together, which has nothing to do with how much they love you. As much as you may wish for your life to be like it used to be, you really need to move on. Once you stop fantasizing and accept the reality, then you can deal with your new life. Try investing some of your creativity in writing or art work that helps you get your feelings out and make you feel good about yourself instead of wasting it on schemes that probably won't get you anywhere.

Sincerely,
Zoe

———————————— Evan's Quick Tips ————

1. If you want to try a "getting them back together" scheme, fall off your bike so that both of your parents have to come to the hospital. (Just kidding!)

2. It's okay to have fantasies, as long as you don't waste too much time living in your head, hoping things will change.

3. Trust that your parents have made a final decision that's right for all of you.

4. Realize that divorce can help everyone in your family get along better.

5. Don't live in the past. Get used to the present and look forward to the future.

What Their Mom Has to Say _____

Most kids have secret fantasies, hopes, and dreams of their parents getting back together. It's hard to believe that they're really going through with this—it takes some time for the reality to sink in. Until it does, you may go back and forth between "getting it" and thinking there's no way this could really be happening. You may get your hopes up, especially if you see your parents laughing, talking, even hugging, and think, "Gee, maybe...." But often parents get along better once they're divorced. This doesn't mean they're going to change their minds.

Why not?

Because if your parents could have worked out their problems, they would have. As much as you love them and wish your family could be the way it used to be, there's nothing you can do to fix their marriage.

It's fine to fantasize for a while. But if, after a few weeks or months, you keep wishing and hoping that your parents will reunite, ask them if there's any real possibility of this happening. If they say "No," take them at their word. Tough as it is, you need to believe that their decision is final.

Your Turn _____

On a scale of 1 to 10, how real does your parents' divorce seem to you?

How often do you fantasize about them getting back together?

Deep down in your heart, do you think there is any chance of this happening?

. . . .

FANTASIES ARE OKAY AS
LONG AS I CAN ACCEPT
REALITY.

. . . .

Stop Trying to Make Me Feel Better 3

IF YOUR PARENTS TELL YOU EVERYTHING WILL BE OKAY OR KEEP TRYING TO MAKE IT UP TO YOU

Zoe: Parents shouldn't say everything will be okay, because they don't really know for sure. Plus, what parents think is okay isn't necessarily what a kid thinks is okay.

Evan: But wait a minute. Sure, it makes you feel better when parents say everything is okay because it's the truth. But sometimes you can't handle them saying it because deep down you don't really believe it. It ticks you off 'cause how do they know? It's kind of ironic—it's true that things will get better, but it doesn't help to hear it.

Zoe: Besides, kids can tell when their parents are trying to smooth things over so that they won't worry. But we're going to worry and it's not necessarily even about what parents think we're worrying about. Like your mom might say, "Everything will work out," thinking you're feeling crummy about the fact that your dad moved out, when really you're feeling bad 'cause you see how sad she is and you wish you could help.

Evan: Yeah, but parents say everything will be okay or try to make it up to you in order to make themselves feel better. Go ahead and let them do it. Parents try so hard and I don't blame them, but the only thing that really helps is time.

Zoe: I agree. Parents lead their kids on, which makes us not trust them. Kids need to know the truth, otherwise we're going to grow up really confused when we get in the real world and have to handle similar situations. Parents can say "It will be okay" all they want or buy you things to cheer you up, but giving your kids gifts is no substitute for giving them your love.

Evan: The bottom line is that nothing really helps. This is something you just have to get through. The only thing that makes it better is when you see for yourself that everything's fine. When kids are scared, hurt, or angry it helps for parents to be calm. Acting so worried only makes kids worry more.

Dear Zoe,

I'm sick of my parents giving me all this b.s. about how everything's going to be fine. I don't happen to feel fine at all at the moment, and whenever they say it I just want to tell them to shut up and leave me alone. I know everything will be fine, but why do they have to say it over and over and over?

Kim, age 14

Dear Kim,

I understand how you feel. Parents keep trying to reassure you because they're freaking out about it, but it just makes you feel pressured, like you have to give them some answer so they'll feel better. You can try asking them to stop and just tell them you're doing fine and would rather not keep talking about it. Assure them that they'll be the first to know if you're having any problems and let them know what would help. Then, be sure to go to them for help. If they don't stop, try to just let it slide off and not get to you. They can't help

——————— Evan's Quick Tips ———————

1. Check out the situation yourself. Decide if you're really doing fine or not.

2. Know that your parents are trying to comfort you.

3. Ask them to give you a little more credit and believe that you can handle this, since you're not a baby and you can handle reality.

4. Let them say what they need to say or give you presents if it makes them feel better.

5. Listen to them, because they're right. In the end, everything will be okay.

What Their Mom Has to Say ——————

Parents sometimes go way overboard trying to reassure kids that everything will be better during and after a divorce. We do this because we care so much—we're worried about you and want to do anything and everything we can to make this easier on you. To be honest, parents may also say "Everything will be okay" to make ourselves feel better. It's normal for us to blame ourselves for the pain and havoc the divorce causes you. But as Zoe and Evan rightfully say, it truly doesn't help for parents to pretend everything's okay when it's not. Doing this might make you feel as if we're not really listening—or respecting—your feelings, which isn't fair.

We may also try to make it up to you with presents or special privileges, which can be a temporary way to help you feel better. But this doesn't solve the problem. Both parents and kids can do something to change this: Parents can learn to let kids feel what they feel without trying to put a "Band-Aid" on the feelings, and kids can try to be honest about what they really feel and need. This is a more realistic and better way for everyone to get through this difficult time.

Your Turn

Take a moment to think about how you are really feeling right now about your parents getting divorced. Now, think about two or three things that might make you feel better.

For example, it may help to get some information by asking your parents about the future. Or you may need them to give you some space and leave you alone for a while until you're more used to the idea. Or it may help to spend more time with your friends.

Think about what you need and then complete this sentence:

Right now, it would help for my parents to _____
_____.

•   •   •   •   •   •   •   •   •   •   •   •   •   •   •   •

I WILL TELL MY PARENTS WHAT WILL HELP TO MAKE ME FEEL BETTER.

•   •   •   •   •   •   •   •   •   •   •   •   •   •   •   •

Where's My Stuff?

WHEN YOU LIVE IN TWO DIFFERENT PLACES

Evan: Basically, kids need a place for everything at both houses and you need to learn how to keep track of your stuff. Otherwise, you end up incredibly frustrated. Last year when I came home from camp, my trunk ended up at Mom's and I still haven't found my favorite shorts. This can be a big problem. Of course, there's a good part, too. When you live in two different places, you learn to be more responsible, which you'll need later when you're grown up.

Zoe: Yeah, but meanwhile, it's a hassle. Sometimes I forget my backpack at Mom's house and then Dad has to drive over there at 10 o'clock at night and he gets really mad. But it's not my fault. I don't drive! I think every set of divorced parents should have a special tube with a button where a little green man delivers the stuff that's left from one house to another.

Sometimes you just end up buying duplicates so you have two of everything. When my parents first got divorced, I used to take my stuff in this blue suitcase from one house to the other and it was a pain in the elbow. I felt like I was going on a trip. Now we've worked it out so that I have most of what I need at both houses. But the good part is it's fun to live at two different houses, 'cause you get to have different lifestyles.

Evan: I agree. Half the time I live in this 100-year-old house with hissing radiators, Jamaican pictures on the walls, and about 29 different chairs. The rest of the time I live in a new apartment with an indoor garage and a pop machine. Luckily, I like both places, but sometimes it would be easier to have one bedroom so I'd know exactly where I live and not have to go back and forth. I feel safer and more secure when most of my stuff is all in one place where I know how to find it.

Zoe: I really feel like I have two homes. When I'm sick, I like to be at Dad's. He always knows where the thermometer is and there's a TV in my bedroom. But I like having my friends come over to Mom's 'cause she hangs out with us and they think she's really cool.

What it really comes down to is getting used to two different homes and making sure you know where you're going to be so you have what you need. You have to work together with your parents so that they tell you exactly what the schedule is, but then you need to remember where you're going and be as responsible as possible.

Dear Zoe,

I have one bike. I like to bike at Mom's house 'cause it's close to the lake, and I like to bike at Dad's house 'cause I have lots of friends in the neighborhood. When Mom picks me up at Dad's, we have to get my bike in and out of Mom's car, which is really a pain. Then, if it ends up at her house and it's my night at Dad's, I either have to ask Dad to go get it or call Mom and ask her to bring it over.

I've told my parents I need a bike at both houses, but they say we can't afford another one right now. I don't want to pressure my parents about getting another bike but I'm really getting frustrated. Any ideas?

Jamie, age 10

Dear Jamie,

Boy, that's rough. Since you're only 10, you're stuck with depending on your parents to schlep your stuff back and forth, which isn't so great. But it isn't the worst thing in the world. You can help by thinking ahead about when you'll really need your bike and asking them nicely to help you bring it back and forth. Obviously, the best solution would be a bike at both houses, but you shouldn't pressure your parents too much. Divorce causes a lot of money problems and they may not be able to afford one.

Here are a few other ideas: You could ask to do some chores around the house so that you can buy a used bike—they can be real cheap at garage sales. You can put a bike at the top of your birthday or Christmas list, so that you know that eventually you'll have one at both places. You could also look around for some used Rollerblades because they're much easier to transport from one house to the other. Another way to solve the problem is to ask your friends to come to your house on the days you don't have your bike. And if all else fails, you might just have to walk.

Yours truly,
Zoe

Evan's Quick Tips

1. Get organized. Make sure you know what you need whenever you switch places.
2. Ask for a weekly written schedule of where you'll be when. This is perfectly reasonable.
3. Put up a checklist of your important things. Before you leave, put a mark next to what you're taking so you won't be caught off guard.
4. Find a central place in your room where you can put all the things that

you normally take back and forth—your backpack, jacket, or favorite CDs—so that it's easy to find them.

5. Ask your parents to help you get the basic stuff you need at both houses.

What Their Mom Has to Say

As Zoe and Evan point out, there are both pros and cons to living in two different places. On the one hand, you're forced to keep better track of your belongings, and at times you may forget something you need—the book you're in the middle of or your stuffed animal—and have to go without it. You have to be extra organized. You may or may not like the living arrangements your parents have made, which is always worth trying to talk with them about.

Although we still struggle at times—Evan ends up at his Dad's without his Rollerblades or Zoe needs her new jeans for a party and they're at the wrong house—we've instituted a few rules that make it easier. Before the kids leave my house, we talk about the plans for the next few days and decide what they will need to bring. If they forget something, they don't have it. But if I forget to remind them, then it's up to me to deliver it, especially if it's something important like a homework assignment that's due the next day. The older Zoe and Evan get, the more responsibility they have for making sure they have what they need.

On the positive side, there are some real advantages to living in two different homes. You might get to have two sets of neighborhood friends. Or you might enjoy having each of your parents' undivided attention when you're with them.

Your Turn _____

What DON'T you like about living in two different places?

What DO you like about living in two different places?

Have you talked to your parents about how you feel about your living arrangements?

Is there anything you can do to make things run more smoothly when it's time for you to make the switch?

. . . .

I AM RESPONSIBLE. I CAN KEEP TRACK OF MY STUFF.

. . . .

It's Not Your Fault 5

IF YOU FEEL GUILTY OR RESPONSIBLE

Evan: This is something grown-ups think is a big deal and worry about, but I seriously don't think most kids have this issue. But if you actually think it's your fault that your parents got divorced, take it from me: It's not. It never was. It never will be. They would have gotten divorced anyway, so quit worrying that it's something you did.

Zoe: You know, that's good advice. But I can see how you might wonder if you had something to do with the divorce, especially if some of your parents' fights had to do with them arguing about stuff like how to raise you or whose turn it is to drive the carpool or whether or not you're old enough to get your ears pierced.

Evan: Yeah, but all parents fight about that stuff. It's really really bad if you feel guilty. You'll always think there's something you could have done, but you have to keep telling yourself that you had nothing to do with it. Of course, you're part of the family and your parents may have argued about things that involve you, but that still doesn't make it your fault. Your parents got divorced because of their differences, not because of anything you did.

Zoe: But even if you know that, you might worry that you could have helped by being better behaved or more cooperative. Still, you have to try to not take this on. Just keep telling yourself, "I didn't cause it. There's nothing I can do to fix it."

Dear Zoe,

My parents are getting divorced and they say it has nothing to do with me or my sister. But I know it's partly my fault. My parents work really hard and are so stressed out trying to make a living and give us everything we need. They come home after work exhausted, and then have to listen to my sister and I fight over stupid stuff like clothes or who gets to use the phone. I've seen that my mom's been really upset and I haven't helped around the house or been very understanding. I feel so bad inside because I know if I had helped more, maybe my parents would still be together.

Rachel, age 13

Dear Rachel,

It's NOT your fault. You may have added to your parents' stress, but their marriage was already in bad shape or they wouldn't be getting divorced. All kids fight and all parents have problems but they don't necessarily get divorced. So don't dwell on how you could have prevented it, because you couldn't have. If you can't stop feeling guilty, ask your parents if you might have done anything wrong, and I'll bet they'll tell you that it isn't your fault. No matter how "bad" you think you've been, you didn't cause your parents to get divorced. They had their own unsolvable problems that had nothing to do with you.

Yours,
Zoe

1. Don't take your parents' problems on your shoulders.

2. Tell your parents how you feel so they can reassure you.

3. If you really feel guilty about having done something bad, just try to be a better kid from now on, which will make you feel good and help make things go more smoothly in your family right now.

4. Give yourself a break.

5. Remember you're just a kid. No kid is responsible for their parents' divorce.

What Their Mom Has to Say _____

Even if your parents tell you over and over that you did nothing to cause their divorce, you may still wonder or worry about whether or not you had anything to do with it. You may have overheard your parents arguing about raising you, disciplining you, whose turn it was to drive the carpool, or whether or not they could afford camp and where the money would come from, which makes you wonder if it's your fault. IT'S NOT! Feeling guilty is a way of searching for reasons that make sense: "Maybe if I'd kept my room clean," "Maybe if I'd been nicer to my brother," "Maybe if I hadn't kept asking my parents to buy me those expensive tennis shoes."

If you keep feeling guilty, repeat to yourself several times a day: "I didn't cause my parents divorce. There's nothing I can do to make it better." Remember: No matter how many times you've screwed up, your parents are getting divorced because they can't get along, not because of anything you've done.

Your Turn _____

Do you feel guilty or responsible for your parents' divorce?

If so, how do you think you contributed to their marriage ending?

Is there something you believe you could have done to prevent it?

Have you asked your parents whether your behavior had anything to do with them deciding to get divorced?

. . . .

I'M NOT TO BLAME FOR MY PARENTS' DIVORCE.

. . . .

Nobody Asked My Opinion 6

IF YOU'RE MAD, SAD, OR SCARED

Evan: When you first find out, it's this whole terrible thing. My parents said that they loved each other and they loved us, but they had to live apart. I felt like, "How could you do this to me?" It was so bad, it was almost indescribable. I didn't want to be around either of my parents. It helped that I had my sister. It's so much easier when there's someone to talk to who feels the same way. Zoe hid her head in the couch and then ran into her room. We cried together and she got me my Raggedy Andy doll.

Zoe: I was so glad we had each other. I was really annoyed at Mom and Dad. I was frustrated that I had to deal with it. I was angry at all the changes that came along with it, like having to move and talk about it. I was embarrassed to be upset. I wanted to be comforted, but I was too mad to let my parents hold me or see me cry.

Evan: It seems like kids should be a little prepared for it since half of all families get divorced. But when it happens to you, it still hurts. It's real and unreal at the same time. Hopefully, your parents will do something to make up for it, like take you to the store and buy you candy. Surprisingly, it made me feel better! When you're that sad and angry, anything that makes you feel better helps.

Zoe: One thing that makes me feel better is that I'm now somebody my friends can talk to when they have problems. Talking about feelings helps, and when your parents go through a divorce, you have to talk about it *so* much. There are other ways, like writing and drawing your feelings, singing your feelings, writing a poem, and writing to your parents. "You've Got a Friend" by Carole King is a good song to listen to.

Evan: Music does help, but what really helps is to remember that the way you feel when you first find out your parents are getting a divorce is not the way you'll always feel. Stuff does change, and after a while you get used to it and realize it's not so awful after all. At first it's kinda tense and nasty, but eventually it gets easier. It seems like your life is over, but really it's just starting in a new way.

Dear Zoe,

My parents just got divorced and I'm really mad at them. I'm scared, too, 'cause I don't know who I'm gonna live with. I don't know what will happen. They keep saying everything's fine, but I'm scared and I feel alone. My parents seem too upset to talk, so I can't ask them right now. Can you help me?

Simone, age 10

Dear Simone,

You're very brave to say how scared you are. Divorce IS scary; you wonder where you'll live, who will take care of you, and if your parents will ever act normal again. But guess what? You're not the only one who feels this way! It helps to talk to someone who understands—a friend, your school counselor, or your parents if they have room to listen.

If you're worried about bothering your parents, remember they're not upset with you, they're just a mess because of what they're going through. And they're probably worried about how you're doing, so don't be afraid to get in there and ask them for what you need.

There are also support groups where you sit around with other kids who are going through the same thing. I highly recommend them.

Best wishes,
Zoe

P.S. Things will improve. I promise.

Evan's Quick Tips

1. Let yourself feel bad. Don't keep your feelings all bunched up inside.

2. Talk to your best friends. Ask them for hugs or make jokes with them. Laughing really helps!

3. Kick something. (No screens—I did that and had to pay for it.) Hit your pillow or throw something that won't break across the room.

4. Write down your feelings in a notebook or journal.

5. Remember this is all new. It takes time to get used to changes.

What Their Mom Has to Say

You're right: It's not fair! Although they certainly took you into account, your parents decided to get divorced without asking your opinion or giving you a vote. Can you remember how you felt when your parents first told you? Were you surprised? Mad? Sad? Scared of what would happen to you? Most kids feel angry, and rightfully so. Even if you believe that your parents made the right decision, you're still stuck having to deal with the fact that they couldn't make their marriage work. You may also feel sad about your parents no longer being together.

As time goes on, your feelings about your parents' divorce will probably change. Little by little, life starts getting back to normal. You may feel relieved not to have to listen to your parents fighting and less sad as you see that everything is turning out all right. But the important thing to know is that whatever you feel is okay to feel. You are entitled to be mad, sad, or angry for as long as it takes. You don't have to keep these feelings locked inside. If you can't share them with your parents, talk to someone else you trust.

Your Turn _____

Does anything about your parents' divorce make you feel angry?

Does anything about your parents' divorce make you feel scared?

Does anything about your parents' divorce make you feel sad?

Who is the one person in your life you feel most comfortable sharing these feelings with?

. . . .

I KNOW THAT MY FEELINGS MAY CHANGE, BUT FOR NOW I HAVE EVERY RIGHT TO BE MAD, SAD, OR SCARED.

. . . .

Quit Putting Me in the Middle

7

IF YOU FEEL LIKE YOU'RE BEING PULLED BETWEEN YOUR PARENTS

Zoe: Lots of times when parents get divorced, the kid gets stuck in the middle. The kid might end up being a "messenger" between the parents. This is wrong. It should stop. This is a parent problem and shouldn't be a kid problem. It makes kids feel used.

Evan: I don't know a lot about this because my parents don't do this. But I think kids should just say "No" if their parents put them in the middle. It's a mess, because you worry about the consequences since you don't necessarily know if you're going to do the right thing. Depending on how responsible the kid is, they could either forget or not give the other parent the message, so it really isn't fair.

Zoe: Here's something else that's not fair: Parents also put kids in the middle by saying mean things about the other parent. This is really awful. Parents shouldn't bash the other parent in front of the kid, because it may get back to the other parent, which is probably why they're saying it in the first place. You want to defend your parent, but you don't want to get in trouble. What are you supposed to say? You love both your parents, so you don't want to hear bad things about them.

Evan: No kidding! Getting put in this position makes kids feel like they're the one who's the problem, especially if the parents are fighting about something involving the kid. It's best to stay out of it, but if you feel like one parent is right, it's okay to say you agree with them. But try not to take sides, because it's bad ethics to choose one parent over the other.

Zoe: That's a no-win situation. When your parents fight in front of you, it makes you feel bad and in the wrong place—you just want to leave, but where's a kid to go? It's scary because you wonder if your parents are defective. If they're still fighting, then it's not just that they were unhappy together—maybe there's something seriously wrong with them. They should be mature enough to get along. I get along with both of them, so why can't they get along with each other?

Evan: One good thing about this is that it helps you realize why your parents got divorced. But it's best to just stay out of the middle.

Zoe: I know divorced parents have conflicts they have to work out, but getting put in the middle of their problems makes you worry about things you shouldn't have to worry about. Parents should communicate with each other, not through their children. Some things are not for kids' ears.

Dear Zoe,

My mom keeps asking me whether my dad is dating anybody. Obviously, she wants me to tell her, but it makes me feel uncomfortable because I know she isn't going to like the answer. I've met my dad's new girlfriend and I don't want to lie to my mother, but I don't want to be the one to tell her in case it causes more problems between my parents. What should I do?

Karen, age 13

Dear Karen,

This is a hard call to make if you're a kid. You sort of can't win either way. You shouldn't have to deal with this, but if it continues you could tell your dad that your mom's been asking if he has a girlfriend and suggest that he tell her so that you don't have to. If you're uncomfortable being the one to tell your mom, then don't do it. If she has questions, tell her to talk to your dad instead of talking to you.

Regards,
Zoe

Evan's Quick Tips

1. Tell your parents that you don't want to take sides.

2. Try to stay in a neutral zone but don't lie to them.

3. If your parents fight in front of you, go to your room and put on loud music or call one of your friends. And remember, they're not fighting about you.

4. Force your parents to deal with each other by flatly refusing to get involved.

5. Suggest they go to counseling and work it out.

What Their Mom Has to Say

Do your parents ever ask you to relay messages, report back on what's going on with your other parent, or say nasty things that you'd rather not hear? The reason parents do this is because they don't know how to communicate with each other or are having trouble dealing with their own anger and pain. But it's totally unfair to you. You should never have to defend one of your parents to the other or worry about whether you're going to get in trouble for messing up by saying the wrong thing. Hopefully, your parents will learn how to deal directly with each other instead of putting you in this awkward position.

In the meantime, Evan suggests, "If one parent calls and tells you to tell your other parent something, just hand them the phone and walk out of the room."

Zoe suggests, "Write your parent a letter explaining how bad it makes you feel when you're put in the middle."

Here's what I suggest: Just say "No!" Any time your parent tries to put you in the middle, say to them, "This is between you and Daddy/Mommy, not between you and me."

Your Turn _____

Do you ever feel as if your parents are putting you in the middle?

If so, how do you feel when this happens?

How can you protect yourself so you don't end up in this position?

• • • • • • • • • • • • • • • • •

I KNOW MY BOUNDARIES AND I CAN KEEP MYSELF SAFE.

• • • • • • • • • • • • • • • • •

Who's in Charge?

DIFFERENT HOUSEHOLDS, DIFFERENT RULES

Zoe: It can be really confusing when you ask your mom something and she says "Yes" and you ask your dad the same thing and he says "No." My dad is stricter than my mom, which sometimes makes me rebel and sometimes I actually like it. It's good because it's nice to have a set of rules so you know what to expect. On the other hand, it's bad because you have to follow the rules, even when they're dumb.

Evan: But guess what, it's not your decision about the rules. Parents are supposed to make the rules—that's what adults are for—if kids made the rules, we'd be running amok. But if your parents are smart, they'll get together on the rules. A lot of this depends on your parents' relationship. If they get along and communicate, it's much easier. But if one says one thing and the other says another thing, then you have to check with both and you don't know what to do. You have to go back and forth telling each of your parents what the other said and you end up obeying the parent who says "No" just to be sure that you don't end up getting in trouble.

Zoe: I stay out of trouble by knowing the rules at each house, which really helps. At Dad's, if our room isn't clean, we can't watch TV. And we only get one hour on the phone on school nights. The good news is that I get more done. But Mom's more flexible and more willing to let me have a say in what's fair. For me, the hardest part is when Dad is strict and I wish Mom was there to rescue me. Sometimes I call and she talks to him; she's pretty good at getting him to compromise.

Evan: Sometimes it would help for your other parent to get in there and be a peacemaker. But for the most part, kids have to work out different rules with each parent and live with them. Different parents have different rules because they're different people—it may be one of the reasons they got divorced. Dad's rules have forced me to budget my time and be more on top of things. But sometimes it's confusing. If one of my parents goes out of town for a week and I end up longer at the other's house, I get used to their rules and then I have to remember new rules again. It's also dangerous when your parents talk to each other about their rules. Mom found out it's my job to vacuum at Dad's and guess what happened?

Zoe: You know, Evan, it doesn't hurt for you to vacuum once in a while. A good way to deal with different rules at different houses is to get your parents together and try to even it out. Your parents might each have to bend a little, but in the end it should turn out pretty well. You might also need to get used to living with one set of rules at one house, and a different set at the other house, like you might have to go to bed at your mom's house at 9 o'clock and your dad's house at 10 o'clock.

Here's a suggestion for how to deal with that: You could read or talk to yourself quietly to keep yourself entertained until 10. Or you could compromise by going to bed at 9:30 at your mom's house….I'm sure your mom would like that. You know, you have some experience with this because you do it on a daily basis. There are different rules at school, at your friends' or grandparents' houses, so just think of it the same way.

Dear Zoe,

I got a referral for getting into a food fight in the school lunchroom and then I got detention for eating popcorn on the bus. It wasn't that big a deal, but I was at Mom's when it happened and she grounded me for a week. I tried negotiating with Dad since I knew he'd give me a warning first before going to such extremes. He said, "When you're at Mom's, she's in charge." Do you think that's fair?

Kim, age 12

Dear Kim,

It doesn't matter if it's fair or not. It's just the way it is. But that doesn't mean there's nothing you can do about it. For example, you can ask your parents for a family meeting to discuss rules and consequences.

I think when it comes to the big things, parents should have some standard operating procedures. If you can get your parents together to discuss this, ask each of your parents to explain their position. Try to get your father to convince your mother that her rules are a bit unreasonable, but be careful because he might end up agreeing with her.

If your parents can't agree, or won't even get together to talk, then you just have to be clear about what the rules are at each house and follow them. You might also stop eating popcorn on the bus or at least try to not get caught.

Take care,
Zoe

———————— Evan's Quick Tips ————————

1. Have a written rule list at each house so you know what to expect.

2. Tell your parents what each others' rules are if they're different.

3. Don't even try to play one parent against the other. It never works.

4. Be flexible. Prepare for temporary rule switches.

5. Before approaching parents on consequences, come up with a really good argument. They might actually listen to your point of view.

What Their Mom Has to Say

Most divorced parents agree on some rules and disagree on others. For example, your dad may think it's fine for you to see a movie rated PG-13, but your mom says "Absolutely no." Your mom may pick up after you, while your dad insists you make your bed and wash your breakfast dishes before leaving for school. One of your parents may let you talk on the phone as much as you want but is very strict about bedtimes, while the other lets you stay up later but considers phone time a privilege you earn once you've completed your chores.

It can be confusing to adjust to different rules each time you switch homes. You can make it easier on yourself by knowing what each of your parents expect of you.

But be careful not to play them against each other. For example, let's say you think your mom is being unfair. Talk to her. Only go to your father with your complaint if you can't get your mom to listen. The same applies if you don't like one your dad's rules.

The best solution is to ask your parents to try to have the same basic standards or to find a middle ground. If that's not possible, then it's up to you to follow each of your parents' rules when you're with them. If you feel they're really unfair or unjust, talk to your school counselor and ask for some feedback on how to handle different rules and expectations.

Your Turn

How are your mom's and dad's rules different?

Do you have different responsibilities at each of their homes?

Do you have different privileges at each of their homes?

Do you feel that each of your parents' expectations are reasonable or unreasonable?

What can you do to adjust to differences in your parents' rules and expectations?

. . . .

I AM FLEXIBLE. I CAN BEND WITH THE WIND.

. . . .

You Never Have Enough Time For Me Anymore 9

IF YOU DON'T GET TO SPEND ENOUGH TIME WITH ONE OF YOUR PARENTS

Evan: My sister and I spend half the time with our mom and half the time with our dad. At the beginning of the month, they meet at my mom's house and work out a schedule. It works out fine, because I get lots of time with each parent. Sometimes I miss being with both of my parents together, but I do get to see them together at school conferences, birthday parties, or when they drop us off or just have coffee together. I can't quite imagine not seeing one of my parents enough…because I love my parents both a lot and want to be with both of them a lot.

Zoe: We're really lucky. But I know other kids who hardly get to spend any time with one of their parents, either because they only get to see their dad every other weekend or because one of them has moved to another city. Although luckily this hasn't happened to me, I can see how it would be really hard. If you don't see one of your parents enough you might worry that they don't love you or don't know what's going on in your life.

Evan: Here's what I don't get: Lots of times, the courts just decide that kids should live with moms, which I think is incredibly stupid and sexist. It should be abolished. If both your parents are good parents, then either one of them can take care of you just fine. But if one of your parents has moved out of town, then there's not much you can do. Sending videotapes back and forth is a good idea. And maybe you can spend summer vacation or special holidays with them. I know a kid who spends his summer with his dad and the school year with his mom. It's fine—basically, after enough time, you can get used to anything.

Zoe: Yeah, but sometimes parents just drift away. I hate to say this, but there are parents who blow it with their kids, either because they're screwed up or have a drinking problem or just can't get their own lives together. Sometimes the reason doesn't matter. If your parent doesn't make an effort to see you, pretty soon you don't want to see them anyway. You may say that you don't care, but obviously you feel dumped and dismissed. It would be great to have both parents in your life, but not if one is hurting you.

Evan: If you end up living most of the time with one parent, you should make sure to spend fun time with the parent you don't see as often. Call them up frequently. Tell them if you want to spend more time with them. If they say "No," ask "Why not?" And keep asking until you get a sufficient answer. If you don't, try calling up the parent you don't see enough and just tell them you're coming for the weekend, whether they like it or not. I mean, they're your parent, they should care about how you feel.

Dear Zoe,

My dad has remarried and it seems as if he never has enough time for me. We make plans and at least half the time he cancels them. He comes up with some stupid excuse, or when he does show up, he brings along his new wife's kids—in which case he may as well not bother seeing me at all. I'm starting to feel as if they're his real family and I've been replaced. Frankly, I don't care if I see him or not. I just wish he'd figure his life out so he'd stop screwing up mine.

Betsy, age 14

Dear Betsy,

Don't give up. You have to believe that your dad loves you even if he's acting like a jerk right now. Tell him how you feel. It's scary to have to say this stuff to a parent, but nobody can help you unless you're willing to tell them the truth. Make sure he knows that you love him and need him to spend time with you, preferably alone. You should try to stay in touch by telephone and get together with your dad even if it means being with his new family. This may not be perfect, but it's a start. It might seem like you're being replaced, but really it's more like being combined. You might try getting close to your stepmom and asking her to help you tell your dad how you feel. But if you try everything and your dad keeps breaking his promises, then you might have to accept that he can't give you what you need. That would be really sad, so give it six months and see if anything improves.

Yours truly,
Zoe

Evan's Quick Tips

1. Talk. If you're upset, tell your parent or somebody else how you're feeling.

2. Call and make a date for just the two of you to do something fun together.

3. Spend some time with your grandparents. I know they're not the same as your parent, but they're family.

4. Get involved in something you like so you're not sitting around waiting.

5. Remember that your parents love you even if they aren't doing a very good job of showing it right now.

What Their Mom Has to Say _____

It's especially hard when divorce keeps you from spending as much time as you want with either of your parents. Unfortunately, when parents get divorced, there are many reasons why they may be less available, either because they've moved out of town, have remarried, or are working harder and have less time. Although you may feel rejected, it's important to remember that if one of your parents isn't around as much, it *doesn't* mean that they don't love you as much as they did before. Of course, knowing this doesn't necessarily make you feel better. It's really okay to feel angry or resentful if you aren't getting the attention or love you need. If you're in this situation, be sure to let your parents know how you feel. It might also help to talk to a friend whose parents are divorced or visit your school counselor and ask him or her to talk to your parents, with or without you. It's hard to be patient, but often this situation works itself out with time. During divorce, life gets a little topsy-turvy, and it can take some time for parents to organize their schedules so that they can be there for their kids. I know it's asking a lot, but try to be as patient as possible.

Your Turn _____

Do you wish you could spend more time with one of your parents? If so, which one, your mom or your dad? Take a moment now to think of a few reasons why either your mom or your dad may be a little less available to you right now.

Next, think about what you might do to improve the situation. For example, you might stay in touch by telephone, set up a special date with that parent, or spend more time with another adult whose company you enjoy.

Now, complete this sentence:

I can try to improve the situation by _____
_____
_____.

. . . .

I'LL TRY TO BE PATIENT AND CREATIVE.

. . . .

Telling Your Friends

10

HOW TO BREAK THE NEWS THAT YOUR PARENTS ARE GETTING DIVORCED

Zoe: You might not know what to say or worry about how your friends will react. You may even feel like a loser or failure—you wish you weren't one of those people who has to say those words: "My parents are getting divorced." But the more people you tell, the easier it gets. Tell your close friends first. Start out slowly or practice in front of the mirror. Or ask a friend to tell some of your other friends.

Evan: That's a good idea, but if you don't want to say anything, wait until you feel comfortable about it. I have a good friend who never even told me his parents were getting divorced. My mom says he must have had some feelings about it, but I think it just wasn't a big deal to him. Frankly, we have better things to talk about, like sports or school or girls.

Zoe: In the beginning, you might not want to have your friends over 'cause it's weird and you feel like you have to explain. But it's better if you do it soon and get used to it. What's really hard is if you're the first one of your friends to go through this. Some stupid friends will say mean things, but just shrug that off, because people who are dumb like that aren't even worth having as friends.

Evan: That's for sure. You shouldn't worry about your friends' reactions. If one of your friends has a problem with it, you just shouldn't hang out with them. And if the parents of one of your friends are going through a divorce, you should be sensitive about how or even whether to bring it up. You can either say something sort of casual and random like "How are you doing?" or else you can just shut up and not bring it up unless they do.

Dear Zoe,

My friends are starting to wonder about what's going on with my parents because my mom's slowing moving out of the house. I want to tell them, but I don't know how and I'm worried about how they'll react. How did you tell your friends?

Mariah, age 10

Dear Mariah,

It was pretty hard for me to tell my friends because it was such a big change. My brother, on the other hand, didn't have any trouble telling his friends. Actually, I'm not sure if he even told anyone. Don't worry about how your friends are going to react. In the long run, all that matters is how you feel about it. If you still feel pretty sad, wait for awhile and maybe just spend more time at your friends' houses so that they don't ask you why one of your parents isn't living there any-more. When you feel ready to talk about it, just do it. Keep it simple, your friends don't have to know all the gory details. You can always just write them a note if you can't find the right words.

Warm wishes,
Zoe

--------------------- Evan's Quick Tips ---------------------

1. Tell the truth. Don't make up any stories.

2. Rehearse ahead of time.

3. Email your friends so you don't have to say it to their face.

4. Wait until you're ready.

5. Don't worry about what your friends think—it doesn't mean anything about you.

What Their Mom Has to Say

If, when, and how you tell your friends that your parents are getting divorced is completely up to you. You needn't feel pressured or in any hurry to talk about it before you're ready. If you do decide to share your news with your friends, you may be very surprised by their reactions. Your good friends will probably not make a big deal about it, and may even give you that hug or word of encouragement that will make you feel a whole lot better.

The whole reason to tell your friends—or anyone else—is to let them in on what's going on in your life so that they can be there for you. If and when the time comes that you care to share this information, choose a friend you really trust. As Zoe recommends, it may help to ask that friend to inform your other friends.

But however you choose to do it, remember that this is your private, personal information and you can share it or keep it to yourself. Do whatever feels right for you.

Your Turn

If, and when, you choose to share the information that your parents are getting divorced, who's the first person you will tell? Take a moment now to think of one or more friends you can trust to respond in the right way and perhaps help you in telling others.

I am thinking about telling _____

_____

_____.

· · · · · · · · · · · · · · · · · · ·

GOING THROUGH DIVORCE IS A
GOOD WAY TO FIND OUT WHO
MY REAL FRIENDS ARE.

· · · · · · · · · · · · · · · · · · ·

I Wish We Were a Normal Family 11

IF YOU EVER FEEL WEIRD OR EMBARRASSED ABOUT BEING FROM A DIVORCED FAMILY

Evan: There's no such thing as normal. Try defining it. Like there's no epitome of smart or pretty or successful. Normal is whatever your life happens to be.

Zoe: Let's get this one thing straight: Being a divorced kid is not abnormal! There is no such thing as normal, except on some of the old-fashioned TV shows our parents used to watch.

Evan: And even those shows were just TV, not real life. Don't wish you were a normal family because every supposed "normal" family has something abnormal about them. Take celebrities or politicians, for example. They seem so perfect but they always have something bad about them written in the paper. I have a friend whose parents are together, but they fight all the time, so what's so great about that?

Zoe: My family seems totally abnormal from the outside. My mom sits around in the middle of the freezing Minnesota winter in cut-offs and a tank top, writing books and playing with our cats, Izzy and Cleo. My dad puts on a suit and goes to work while his boy-friend cleans the house and goes grocery shopping. So don't tell me about normal.

Evan: We're not abnormal, we're just a little funky. If there's one thing I've learned, it's to not compare your family to other families. These days at least half the families are divorced so I'd say you're not really in the minority. I know it used to be a big awful thing when people got divorced, but now it's totally normal. Like five years ago, it was really unusual to have a CD player and now almost everyone has one. Life has changed and it's really not that big a deal.

Zoe: Besides, what feels abnormal might just be a matter of getting used to something new, which is always hard. Even though you know there's nothing to be embarrassed about, you may still feel sad when you see other friends of yours whose parents are together. You shouldn't envy your friends whose parents aren't divorced, but it helps a lot to spend time with friends whose parents are so that you can talk about it and realize you're not alone.

Dear Zoe,

Sometimes I'm jealous that my best friend's parents aren't divorced and mine are. I know there's nothing wrong with being divorced, but when I go over to her house and see them all sitting together at the dinner table, I feel a little sad. It also embarrasses me when her parents or other people ask me who I live with and I have to tell them that I go back and forth between my parents. Do you ever feel this way?

Alex, age 12

Dear Alex,

To be perfectly honest, there are times when I feel a little weird about my parents being divorced, but most of the time I'm pretty okay with it. But I think that's because I've had five years to get over feeling embarrassed and have had lots of experience now with other kids whose parents are divorced. It does help to spend time with other kids in the same situation, as well as kids in "traditional" families so that you can get a taste of different worlds. But don't cut off your best friend because she can probably help you with some of your feelings. Remember: Her life isn't perfect either. For all you know, she envies you for getting to live in two different places.

And never, never let anyone make you feel as if there's something wrong with you because your parents are divorced. If anything, it just makes you unique.

Warm wishes,
Zoe

Evan's Quick Tips

1. Figure out the ways in which your family is like other families.

2. Ask your friends what their families are like.

3. Create a school support group for "abnormal families."

4. Remember it's cool to be different.

5. Watch reruns of The Brady Bunch.

What Their Mother Has to Say

When I was growing up, kids whose parents were divorced really were in the minority. But as Zoe and Evan point out, that's no longer the case. In fact, when we wrote this portion of the book, they were surprised that any kid whose parents are divorced would feel abnormal, since over half of the kids they know are in the very same situation.

But numbers don't really mean that much. For example, you can feel embarrassed if you have zits or a bad haircut, even if lots of other kids at school have zits or a bad haircut, too. Often when we say we don't feel "normal," what we mean is that "I feel like I stand out." Or "I feel different than everyone else." It's natural to feel this way, especially in the beginning stages of divorce, when lots of people—your parents, friends, or school counselors—may bring up your parents' divorce, which can make you feel uncomfortable or embarrassed. The best way to deal with these feelings is by spending time with other kids whose parents are also divorced. But here's something interesting: It's just as important to spend time with your usual friends, some of whose parents aren't divorced, which will remind you that some things are still the same. Most of all, remember that you're still the same person, even though your life has changed and will continue to do so.

Your Turn _____

Make a list of every single kid you know whose parents are divorced. Make plans to spend time with at least one of the kids on your list.

Make a list of your friends whose parents aren't divorced. Make plans to spend time with at least one of the kids on this list.

. . . .

I HAVE NOTHING TO BE ASHAMED OF. I'M PROUD OF BEING WHO I AM.

. . . .

I Don't Want to Meet Your Boyfriend

12

WHEN YOUR PARENTS START TO DATE

Evan: Watching your parents date can be pretty awkward. When you first meet someone your mom or dad is going out with, of course you don't like them. Actually, you just don't like the idea of them being around. They're strange, and you assume they kind of want to take the place of your other parent, which they never could.

Zoe: I agree, but even so, you feel protective of your parents. You don't want them to get hurt and have to go through another divorce. My mom was involved with someone and I really liked him and then they broke up, which made me mad that I'd even bothered to get to know him. It also can be creepy when your mom or dad start getting romantic. If your parent comes home from a date and you're watching from the bedroom window and they're sitting in a car for a half hour and you know what they're doing, it makes you feel weird.

Evan: You don't have to watch! And anyway, actually, you get used to it. And after a while, it's kind of good. When Mom first met her new boyfriend, I didn't even want him around. He'd come over to watch basketball with me and I knew he was just trying to get on my good side, so Mom would like him more. But now I like him, too. He's a Mister Fix-It and drives us to school if Mom is sick. He's nice and my friends like him too.

Zoe: This can go one of two ways: Your parents can meet someone you really like, but they can also fall in love with someone you can't stand, which can turn into a major disaster. It's awful when you end up stuck having to hang out with and be nice to someone you really can't stand, either because they're wrong for your parent or they're not very nice to you. Even when they pretend they like you, you know they're just trying to get on your good side. But there can also be some advantages to your parents dating: When my friend Jason's dad met a woman after going through a divorce, he got a lot nicer. He was happier, so he was better to his kids. The same's true of Mom. I like it that she has someone who cares about her and makes her feel loved. Plus, I don't want her to end up being an old lady all alone.

Evan: C'mon, can you really imagine Mom all alone? Anyway, getting used to your parents dating is another one of those things that takes time. It's like when you eat a pastry, you've got to get through the crust to get to the gooey part. If you get to know somebody, you usually find something to like about them, unless they're a jerk, in which case your parent will figure that out. You just have to trust your parents to find someone good and then do your best to get along with them.

Dear Zoe,

My parents got divorced a few months ago and now my dad has a new girlfriend. I'm only at my dad's on the weekends and she's always there. I like her okay, I just wish she wasn't there every time I'm with my dad. He acts different, and I can tell he's nervous because he keeps asking me what I think of her. I really don't care if he has a girlfriend, I just wish it could be the two of us like it used to be.

Mark, age 9

Dear Mark,

You have every right to tell your dad how you feel. Here's how to do it: Start by telling him you like his girlfriend (If it's a lie, think about one thing about her that doesn't make you sick.) Then, tell him you miss him and want some time alone with him. Suggest a compromise. Maybe she can join you on Saturday afternoon, but the rest of the time you'd like his undivided attention.

This is NOT too much to ask. If he refuses, tell him that you'll end up liking his girlfriend more if you don't have to spend the whole week-end with her. That usually works. You're being totally reasonable about your dad having a girlfriend and your dad should be equally reasonable about spending time with you alone.

Peace,
Zoe

Evan's Quick Tips

1. Be polite. You don't have to like your parent's girlfriend or boyfriend, but you do have to be civil.

2. Have an open mind. Most people have a good side if you give them a chance.

3. Know that no one can replace your parents. Ever.

4. Be honest about how much time you want to spend with this person.

5. If you're uncomfortable, invite a friend over so you don't have to be alone with your parent's new boyfriend or girlfriend.

What Their Mom Has to Say _____

After seeing your parents together your whole life, it can feel strange to see them dating. You may or may not like this new person who has suddenly appeared on the scene. You may resent them being around. You may worry about how to act around them or feel pressured to be nice. You may be totally grossed out if you see them holding hands, kissing, or acting all mushy. Mostly you may worry that your mom or dad will marry this person and you'll be stuck with them forever. On the other hand, you may really like who your parent is dating and feel excited about them having met someone new. Whether you like them or not, the fact is, your parents are adults and have the right to date.

But you have the right to hold back until you're sure of how you feel and have some say in how involved you want to be. A good way to start is by thinking of two or three things you like about the person your mom or dad is dating. Next, think about the parts that make you uncomfortable and tell your parent how you really feel. You might say something like, "I think your new boyfriend's okay, but I really don't want to know any details about your relationship" or "For now, I'm not ready to spend time with the two of you."

And be sure to ask any questions on your mind, such as, "Is this person going to move in with us?" "How serious are you?" or "Are you going to get married?" The more information you get, the less you'll have to worry about what might or might not happen.

Your Turn _____

List two or three things you really like about the person your parent is dating.

Now, list two or three things you don't like about the person your parent is dating.

Finally, think about one way in which you can create a better rela-

tionship with this new person in your life, for example, by spending time alone with him or her, taking more time to get to know them, or talking to your parent about your concerns.

Then, complete this sentence:

I can try to get along better with my parent's boyfriend or girlfriend by _____
_____.

. . . .

IF MY PARENT LIKES THIS PERSON, I CAN GET TO LIKE HIM OR HER, BUT I CAN TAKE MY TIME DEVELOPING MY OWN RELATIONSHIP.

. . . .

Let's Have My Birthday Party at the Mall

13

DEALING WITH BIRTHDAYS, HOLIDAYS, AND OTHER SPECIAL OCCASIONS

Zoe: Birthdays and holidays are like a trip down memory lane. They can make you feel sad because they remind you of what it was like when you were all together as a family. You have to get used to changing traditions. If your family is used to having this big bash together and now you can't, then you may have to spend some time with one side of your family and other occasions with the other side, instead of being with all your relatives together like you're used to.

Evan: It's great when some parents still manage to spend some holidays together. But others have moved on with their lives and it may just not work anymore to celebrate Thanksgiving or Hanukkah together, so you just have to go with whichever parent you're with. But birthdays are a little different, so parents should make more effort even if they don't want to see each other at those times of the year.

Zoe: You're right. This is one situation in which parents should act like grown-ups. Since you're probably not going to get two birthday parties, your parents should just act like adults and figure out how to spend three hours together to make your birthday nice. Birthdays are a time for kids to be happy—they shouldn't have to deal with family conflicts on what should be a special day. My parents have always gotten together for my birthdays. I know it probably makes them feel both happy and sad, since my birthday must make them think about when they were married and happy, at least when they made me. Of course, it also helps all of us remember that we're still a family because of what we share.

Evan: If it's at all possible, you should get to decide where it would be more fun to have your birthday party because it's YOUR birthday. The same is true for holidays. But you should think about your parents' feelings and not disregard them. Try not to favor one parent over the other, even if you're mad at one of them, because you're still their child. Our parents rotate being in charge of our birthday party every other year, but the other one usually at least shows up for a while. We spend some holidays together and some apart.

If parents can find a way to get it together, great, but if they really can't get along, you're much better off celebrating separately. Sometimes this works to your advantage because you end up with more presents, but not all the time.

Dear Zoe,

Last year my parents made a birthday party for me together. It sucked. They argued the whole time, and my mom got mad at my dad for forgetting to bring the ice cream. They embarrassed me in front of my friends and pretty much ruined my party. Could you please help me with some ideas on how to make it better next year?

Matt, age 11

Dear Matt,

A good idea is to talk to your parents before it's time for your birthday party. They do care, even though it may seem as if they don't. Tell them how it makes you feel when they fight in front of you and your friends. They might even need your help and suggestions on how to get along if they're mad at each other.

If they just can't figure out how to handle it, here's a few ideas on how to have a successful party anyway. Your mom could have the party at her house and your dad could stop by for a couple of minutes and say "Hi." Your parents could take turns having your party every other year. Or you could have two parties, one with each parent, or if that's too expensive, just have two birthday cakes on two different nights.

Whatever you do, don't let your parents ruin your birthday. It's your special day and you deserve to have fun.

Happy Birthday!
Zoe

Evan's Quick Tips

1. Tell your parents what kind of party you want.

2. Take into account everyone's feelings.

3. Have your party at a public place where your parents might not fight.

4. Plan the party yourself and invite both your parents.

5. Get used to celebrating separately because the longer your parents are divorced, the less time you'll spend together for birthdays and holidays.

What Their Mom Has to Say _____

Your birthday is your special day and you deserve to have it be everything you hope for. But unfortunately, it's not always easy for divorced parents to set their differences aside so as to celebrate their children's birthdays—and other holidays—in a peaceful way. Some divorced families are able to celebrate together, some trade off every other year. And there are families that make two parties, in which case, you really luck out.

If your parents are unable or unwilling to celebrate your birthday together, there are a few things you can try to improve the situation. As Evan suggests, you can ask your parents to rise above the situation and make a special effort to get along on your birthday. If they can't, then you're better off having separate celebrations, so that your birthday isn't ruined by tension or fighting between your parents.

The same goes for holidays. As the years pass, it's unlikely that your parents will continue to celebrate Christmas, Hanukkah, or Easter as a family, in which case, you will need to get used to splitting up the holidays. There are pros and cons to this arrangement: On the one hand, you will have to adjust to new traditions. On the other hand, you may gain some new friends and family members in the bargain. While you may always feel a little sad about celebrating birthdays or holidays without both your parents present, this is just another thing to get used to, which gets easier over time.

Your Turn _____

Take a moment to complete this sentence:

Since getting divorced, in my family we celebrate my birthday and other special occasions by _____

_____

_____.

Next, check one of the following:

❏ *I like the way things are.*

❏ *I wish things were different.*

If you checked the second box, complete the following sentence:

On my birthday and other holidays, I'd like my parents to _____

_____

_____.

Are you willing to ask for what you want?

. . . .

I DESERVE TO CELEBRATE MY SPECIAL DAYS WITHOUT WORRYING.

. . . .

Where I'd Rather Live

14

IF YOU WISH YOU COULD CHANGE YOUR LIVING SITUATION

Zoe: It's normal for kids to feel more comfortable with one parent than the other. You might like one better or just get along more easily. But you may not have the choice. I've gone back and forth on this. Sometimes I wish I had more say about where I live, and other times I'm just fine with my parents' custody arrangements.

Evan: Personally, I think kids should be able to choose which parent they live with, but apparently that isn't the way it works. You still might have some power to change things a little. Don't say, "I like you more than Daddy/Mommy so can I live with you?" Instead say, "I just like staying there more. No offense to either of you, it's just the entire atmosphere." Be sure they know it doesn't have to do with not liking that parent, because your parents have a lot of other things on their minds and they shouldn't have to worry about who you like better.

Zoe: A good way to deal with this—and I've done this myself—is to give your parents good, valid reasons why you would be better off spending more time at one or the other's house. For example, maybe it's easier to get your homework done there, or maybe it's in a neighborhood within walking distance of more of your friends. They may see it differently once they know the reasoning behind your requests, but it probably won't make much difference unless you're at least 11 years old.

Evan: I disagree. No matter how young you are, you have the right to express your preference. Most of the time, it won't change the ratio of how much time you spend at one place rather than the other—especially if your parents went to court and some judge decided that it's better for you to stay with one parent more than the other. But it's still worth a try to ask for what you want.

Zoe: Maybe, but since you might not be able to pick where you live, you just have to learn to alter your habits. But don't give up on trying to improve the situation. If you have trouble with one of your parents, tell them what's wrong and what would make it better. You might not like the way your room is, or that they're always on the phone, or you don't like the food, or their house may not be close to where your friends live. Or you might not like the rules if they're more strict. You might ask the parent you get along with better to talk to the other one with you to try to make things better.

Dear Zoe,

I don't want to hurt my mom's feelings, but I like it much better at my dad's house. It's where I lived before they got divorced and now she lives in an apartment that doesn't feel at all like home. How can I tell Mom I'd rather spend more time at Dad's without her thinking I don't love her as much as him?

Alison, age 10

Dear Alison,

You probably can't change the schedule, since that's the sort of thing parents decide without asking you. What you can do is talk to your mom and ask if you might spend a little more time at Dad's, but be sure to tell her why. Tell her you love her, that it has nothing to do *with liking your father more. If she says "No," here's a few other things to try: Bring some of your favorite things to your mom's house so it feels more like home. And when you go to your mom's, take a few minutes ahead of time to say good-bye to your bedroom and your stuff so that the move doesn't feel so hard. You also should give yourself some time to get used to living at your mom's, because the more time you spend there, the more it will feel like home.*

Sincerely,
Zoe

Evan's Quick Tips

1. Think it over before you talk to your parents. Write your reasons down.
2. Figure out what you like at one home and see if you can duplicate it at the other.
3. Try to cope by making it more livable. (For instance, have some of your favorite things around or make new friends in the neighborhood.)
4. Try to negotiate a little more time at the place you prefer.
5. Go to camp.

What Their Mom Has to Say

I'd bet that most kids, given the chance, would prefer to spend more time with one parent than the other. This is perfectly natural. You may feel more comfortable, get along better with, or have more freedom at one parent's home than the other's. But as Evan says, kids rarely get to choose how much time they spend with each parent. And while it may not seem fair to you, parents have their own reasons for how your living time is split up. The living arrangements your parents have set up may be based on their work schedules, location, money concerns, or many other considerations.

Your parents may or may not be flexible about changing your living arrangements, but you are entitled to express your opinion and ask for what you want. If you do, be sensitive to your parents' feelings. Tell them your preferences without making them feel as if you don't like them or don't want to spend time with them.

The good news is that the older kids get, the more say they usually have in who they spend most of their time with. For the time being, it's useful to think of all the ways you can feel better about where you're living, until you're older and can have more influence over it.

Your Turn _____

If it was completely up to you, what living arrangements would you make?

Is there anything about your current living situation that you wish you could change?

Think about one or two ways that you would like to make improvements, then complete this sentence:

I would like to change _____
_____.

I can be happier and more comfortable where I am by _____
_____.

• • • • • • • • • • • • • •

THERE'S NO PLACE LIKE HOME.

• • • • • • • • • • • • • •

You're Not My Father

LEARNING TO LIVE WITH STEPPARENTS

Zoe: When you first get a stepparent, it's pretty uncomfortable because you don't know how you're supposed to act around them or what you're supposed to call them. Should you call them Mom, Stepmom, a special name, or by their name? You don't know where you stand with them or where they stand with you. You didn't pick them, so you don't know if you really like them or they really like you. If they're horrible, you need to tell your parent. Your parent has the right to find love, but you have the right to be treated well.

Evan: Keep in mind that they're not your biological parent, but they care a lot for you, or at least they should. If they don't, your parent shouldn't be with them. You should try to form a relationship with them. The best thing is to forget they're your "stepparent" and just think of them as a loving adult, like an uncle, who lives with you.

Zoe: It's important for a stepparent to know how much authority they have, so they know when to step in and when not to. I think they should have 40 percent authority, and if they're the only one home they should enforce rules but not make them. Your parents should tell both you and them exactly what's what. In the beginning, they should have about the same authority as a baby-sitter.

Evan: Uh-uh, Zoe. I disagree. They should have more say than a baby-sitter, but they shouldn't have as much authority as your natural parent. And they definitely should have more authority than your older sister! If you don't like them, tough. Your parent loves them, but your parent loves you, too, so you should tell them how you feel, but try to not make your parent feel guilty. I happen to really like my father's new partner. Things are a gizzillion times better since he moved in. He knows a million things, he's a great cook, and he takes really good care of me when I'm sick.

Zoe: Another good thing is that if you're not getting along with your parent, the stepparent can step in (get the pun?) and try to get your parent to listen. They're a bystander, so they can see both sides.

Evan: You just have to give this person a chance. If your parent married him or her, there must be something good about them. If not, your mom or dad will figure it out for themselves.

Dear Zoe,

I know I'm supposed to like my stepmother, but I don't. She's mean and she's nothing like my mom. I don't want to tell my father 'cause he'll get mad and just tell me to get along with her. What am I supposed to do?

Laura, age 11

Dear Laura,

Don't expect to like your stepmother right away. There's no such thing as instant love, it always takes time to get to know someone. Don't expect her to be like your mom. No one can replace your mom, but this woman can be a cool figure in your life. At 11, this may not seem like much, but when you're a teenager, you'll like having another woman in the house. Of course, if she's really mean, tell your dad. He might side with her, but hopefully he'll listen to you. You won't be able to change her living with you, but you can at least give her the benefit of the doubt and hope she cares enough about

Evan's Quick Tips

1. Have a positive attitude.

2. Assume your stepparent is a nice person and wants to get to know you.

3. Spend time doing something special with them. (I went to a basketball game with my mom's boyfriend, which really helped us bond.)

4. Cut them some slack. This must be hard for them too.

5. Make sure you know how much authority they have.

What Their Mom Has to Say

Getting used to a stepparent is another one of the adjustments you have no say in, yet affects your life in so many ways. To put it bluntly, you're stuck with this person. Just because your mom or dad has chosen a new partner, doesn't mean you are happy to have him or her in your life. Some kids are really pleased about having a stepparent, but others resent him or her for lots of different reasons. You may not like the way your stepparent treats you or your parent. You may feel as if they are taking too much of your mom's or dad's time and attention, or you may think they have too much authority. After all, why should some "stranger" have the right to make rules or be in charge of you? All of these issues need to be worked out with your mom or dad, but your parents can only help if you let them know your feelings.

The best way to get results is to ask for what you want. For example, maybe you don't think it's fair for a stepparent to discipline you, or perhaps you'd like to spend at least one night a week with your parent without their new partner. Try not to worry about hurting your parents' feelings when you are being honest about how you feel.

It's also important for you to try to be open to your stepparent. It takes time to get to know anyone new, and more time to develop trust. Your stepparent probably wants you to like him or her and is anxious to find ways to have a good relationship with you. This is a two-way street and you have to be willing to do your part.

Your Turn _____

Think of two or three things you like about your stepparent. For example, "I like it when my new stepmom takes me shopping." Or "My dad is nicer and more patient since he remarried."

Next, think of two or three ways in which you wish your relationship with your stepparent was different. For example, "I wish he'd stop trying so hard." Or "I don't like the way he tells me what to do."

Now, think of one or two ways in which YOU can improve your relationship with your stepparent. For instance, by telling him or her how you feel. Or by finding an activity the two of you can share. Then, complete this sentence:

I can create a better relationship with my stepparent by _____
_____.

• • • • • • • • • • • • • • • • •

I'LL TRY TO LET THIS NEW PERSON INTO MY LIFE.

• • • • • • • • • • • • • • • •

Why Are You Making Me Go to That Stupid Support Group?

16

WHAT SORT OF SUPPORT DO KIDS REALLY NEED?

Zoe: Sometimes it's really perturbing when your parents make you go to a support group or a feelings doctor, which is what my parents called it when I was younger. You have to go and listen to all these people have all these sad feelings, which only makes you feel worse. But it also helps you know that you're not the only one feeling this way.

Evan: I hate to disagree with you, but I don't think support groups help at all. Kids usually don't want to go to a support group, because they feel uncomfortable or think they don't need to go. Telling the story of your parents' divorce and talking about it makes you feel stupid. Personally, I don't like the idea of a bunch of kids talking to each other unless they're really good friends. As far as therapy, why throw away good money talking to someone who just sits there? You may as well talk to Mr. Potato Head! And why should you take their advice? I didn't do it…and I'm fine, right?

Zoe: Well, that's questionable. No, really, I went to a support group that was fun, because I got to get out of class. But my parents made me go to a counselor who I hated going to because she just sat there and I felt embarrassed and wanted to scream "Go away! Don't think that you can make my life better!" But now that I'm 15, I've asked my mom to find me a therapist so that I can talk to someone about what's going on with me.

Evan: So maybe you're the one who needs a therapist! Frankly, I think it's the parents who need to go to a support group or therapy, but instead they make something up about how the kids need support so they'll feel better. It's all an excuse. If you can't talk to your parents, then talk your friends, talk to your teachers who know you and have something useful to offer. If your parents make you go to a therapist, have them go, too.

Zoe: More than anything, kids need support from their parents. We need reassurance that our parents love us and that the divorce wasn't because of us. And we need support from friends who we can talk with about anything without feeling judged. Kids always want to do it themselves, but from going through divorce, I've learned that this is something you can't handle all alone. You have to let other people help.

Dear Zoe,

I'm really unhappy and I don't have anyone to talk to. There's a support group at our church, but I'd be too embarrassed to go. I don't want other people to know that my family has problems and I'm scared what I say would get back to my parents and I'd get in trouble. Any suggestions?

Frank, age 13

Dear Frank,

Just because your family has problems doesn't mean that your family IS a problem. The problem is that you won't talk about it. Try not to be so embarrassed, because everyone has problems. I'd suggest trying the support group. It's hard to talk at first, so you can just listen until you feel comfortable. You can learn a lot, and make some friends, too. At least go and try it; if you don't like it, try it once

---

more, and if it still doesn't feel right, at least talk to one of your friends about what's going on. It always helps to get things off your chest.

Yours truly,
Zoe

Evan's Quick Tips

1. Kids should be asked—not told—how they feel.
2. The only thing good about having feelings cooped up inside is getting them out.
3. Realize that all your feelings are okay.
4. Get lots of love from your parents.
5. If you have to go to a therapist or support group, try to have fun and get something positive out of it.

What Their Mom Has to Say

One of the best things about having two children is that you often get two different opinions on the same topic. On this subject, I agree with both Zoe's and Evan's points of view. Going to a support group with other kids in the same situation can be very comforting. You don't have to talk—just listening to what other kids feel and how they are coping can really help you feel less alone and give you lots of good ideas for how to get through this difficult transition. On the other hand, as Evan says, often parents force kids to go to support groups or see a counselor because they are worried or feel guilty about their kids' suffering as a result of divorce.

If you're not sure whether you need help, here are a few ways to tell: If you are having trouble eating or sleeping. If you're fighting with your friends or parents, or getting in trouble at school. If you feel very sad, angry, or depressed. Kids should only be given professional support if they want it and feel it would help. Besides, there are other ways to deal with this: Talking to friends, writing in a journal, or listening to music can also make you feel better.

But here's one thing to think about: Sometimes we don't try something because we don't know what to expect. And when we don't know what to expect, we may be afraid to try something new. So if you're curious at all, it may be worthwhile to attend a support group or see a counselor once, so you can make up your mind for yourself. You may be pleasantly surprised or you may decide this isn't for you at all. But it won't cost you anything to give it a try.

Your Turn _____

Although you may feel very alone right now, in fact, there are many people in your life who are willing and able to give you the love and support you deserve. Take a moment now to think about what kind of support you would like. (If what you really want is for everyone to leave you alone for a while, that's okay, too.) But if you are open to the idea, think about a couple of people—family, friends, or professionals—you trust enough to share your feelings with right now.

Then, complete this sentence:

It might help to talk to _____.

. . . .

I CAN TRY TO LET OTHER PEOPLE BE THERE FOR ME.

. . . .

I Don't Want Another Sister 17

DEALING WITH BLENDED FAMILIES

Zoe: This kind of situation could be really cool if the kid is really cool, or it could be horrible if the kid is a brat. For example, I always wished I had a big brother or sister to hang out with, but what if I didn't like them? The problem with divorce is that there are all sorts of unknowns. You can end up with a real winner or you can end up having to live with someone you can't stand. (Of course, this can happen with your natural brother or sister, too.)

Evan: I hope you're not referring to me. Anyway, having a stepsibling is something you should try to get used to, because you're stuck with them and they're never going to go away. You just have to treat them as if they're your immediate brother or sister. You don't have to like them—a lot of kids don't like their "real" brother or sister, but that's life. Of course, they could always turn out to be your best friend.

Zoe: Even so, you might also not like sharing your parent with them. If your new sister or brother gets really close to your mom or dad, you feel afraid that they'll start loving them more than you. You want to know that you're still their "real" kid. The flip side would be just as bad. If your parent and your stepsiblings don't get along, then you end up with more fighting in your house, which is exactly what you were hoping to get away from when your parents got divorced.

Evan: Even if you like your new sister or brother, you always feel bad at first because it's different—it's a change. People feel uncomfortable when things change. But after being in a new situation for a while, it gets easier. Like if you break your leg, it's harder to walk and you have to get used to it. But after a while the cast goes away, your leg heals and goes back to normal.

Zoe: If you have a stepsister or stepbrother you don't like, it may be just that you don't know them yet. Spend some time doing something with them you both like, and you might find something in common. Remember: They might not like you just as much as you don't like them, so be nice, tough it out, and they might grow on you over time.

Dear Zoe,

My mother has remarried and now I have a stepbrother who's two years younger than I am. I have to share a room with him, which I really don't appreciate. He hangs out with all my friends, he gets into all my stuff, and he's really getting on my nerves. I want to tell him nicely to get out of my face. How can I do this without causing a whole big family fight?

Jeremy, age 13

Dear Jeremy,

I understand where you're coming from because I have a little brother and even though he's not a stepbrother, he still gets into all my stuff. You need to make some rules, especially since you're sharing a room. Explain which of your belongings he can touch and what's off-limits. If there are some things you don't care as much about, tell him so that he doesn't feel totally shut out of your stuff and your life. Try to include him once in a while with your friends, but don't feel like you have to have him glued to you, which just isn't fair.

You might have to spend more of your time with friends at their houses for a while. If you try all this and it doesn't work, ask your parents to intervene and help out a little bit.

Sincerely,
Zoe

——————Evan's Quick Tips——————

1. Get on a sports team with one of your newly acquired brothers or sisters.
2. Make the first move by being nice to them.
3. Don't judge a book by its cover. Get to know what's inside.
4. Talk to them. Remember, they might have some of the same feelings.
5. Try to spend more time at your other house, if you have one, so the change is more gradual.

What Their Mom Has to Say ——————

Once again, this is one of the parts of divorce in which you have no say, yet which affects you in a big way. If one of your parents remarries you may end up with new sisters or brothers, which can be terrific, terrible, or something in between. This is another situation in which you have to make changes whether you like it or not.

If your stepbrother or stepsister is mean, annoying, or disrespectful toward your belongings, you should definitely express your opinions and feelings to your parent. You will no doubt need to compromise, especially if you're sharing a bedroom. But on the positive side, your new stepsibling may bring some wonderful books, toys, or computer games along, not to mention new friends you may really like. If you're an only child, you may end up with the brother or sister you've always wanted, and if you only have a same-sex sibling, you might get one of the opposite gender.

It's very important to remember that your stepsibling is probably experiencing a similar adjustment, so you have lots in common. Your willingness to have a positive attitude can make a big difference in how you end up feeling toward your stepbrother or stepsister.

Your Turn

If you've "inherited" a stepbrother or stepsister, how do you feel about him or her?

Do you resent your stepsibling or are you happy to have him or her in your life?

There's almost always something to like about every person, if you really think about it. So begin now by thinking of something you might really like—or get to like—about this person:

One thing I like or could get to like about my stepsibling is _____
_____.

Next, come up with a few ideas on how you can create a good relationship with him or her:

I can improve my relationship with my stepsibling by _____
_____.

• • • • • • • • • • • • • • •

I'LL TRY TO HAVE AN OPEN MIND AND AN OPEN HEART.

• • • • • • • • • • • • • • •

Is There Any Such Thing as a Happy Marriage?

18

DOES LOVE EVER LAST?

Zoe: My mom once promised me that she'd never get divorced, and she did. That just goes to show you that marriage is risky business, which you've probably already figured out. Kids whose parents get divorced might have some fears if marriage can work or not. Yes, it can. Your parents probably just haven't found the right person to marry.

Evan: It's really wonderful when they do. Marriage is something that happens when two people love each other so much they want to spend the rest of their lives together. In many relationships, that feeling or some of that feeling goes away for a while. But not everybody gets divorced.

Zoe: Just because my mom got divorced doesn't mean I will. Even though my parents aren't together anymore, they're still friends; you can still be close if you're not married. Most kids' only experience with marriage is their own parents, so they think, "Well they couldn't make it work, so nobody can." But lots do.

Evan: If you grow up and make a commitment to somebody, don't sit around worrying about losing your love for them. Have a marriage where you expect and accept the ups and downs. Don't be afraid of getting divorced. If it happens, it happens. I'm really not conscious of being afraid of getting married, but who knows? Maybe my "inner child" is afraid of getting into a relationship when I'm older, but I don't think so. Maybe subconsciously we're all a little afraid. But at this point, I'm certainly willing to take my chances.

Dear Zoe,

My boyfriend and I haven't been getting along for the past month. We fight a lot and I think I should break up with him, but my friends all say that he's great and I shouldn't dump him unless I'm totally sure. But how do you be totally sure? I don't want to end up in a relationship like my parents', where you fight all the time and then end up breaking up anyway. I love him, but I'm scared of getting hurt. What do you think I should do?

Carly, age 15

Dear Carly,

I think that you have to take a chance on love. It's true that all relationships have problems and everyone fights with their boyfriend or girlfriend. Since you're just 15, you'll probably have lots of other relationships, and all of them will have some problems, but that's no reason to be scared. Just because your parents' marriage didn't work out doesn't mean that yours won't.

And even if you end up breaking up with your boyfriend, just because something ends doesn't mean it was a bad relationship. You still got a lot out of it. So don't get all stressed out about what might happen in the future. Just do your best to make this relationship work and if it doesn't, there's always someone new.

Have courage,
Zoe

1. Not everyone gets divorced.

2. There are lots of different reasons why people get divorced. Find out why.

3. Learn from your parents' mistakes.

4. Talk to grown-ups whose marriages have lasted.

5. Take risks.

What Their Mom Has to Say _____

Parents should try never to lie to their kids about anything. And believe me, as I've told Zoe many, many times, I shouldn't have made a promise I couldn't keep. But I meant it at the time. That's one of the hardest things about saying "I do." When we make the commitment to marry another person, we mean it from the bottom of our heart, but unfortunately, things don't always work out. Everyone gets hurt, and one of the ways kids sometimes get hurt is that they start wondering whether love can truly be forever and whether it's possible for any marriage to make it long term.

As a parent, I sometimes wonder and worry whether my divorce has caused Zoe and Evan to think that marriage is an outdated or impossible ideal. Many parents—and many experts—think that divorce may cause kids to be scared of getting involved in love relationships once they're grown up. But according to what my kids say, these may be unnecessary concerns. I'm glad and relieved that Zoe and Evan, and hopefully other kids as well, realize that just because their parents got divorced, this doesn't mean they will do the same someday.

In fact, just the opposite may be true. Maybe, just maybe, kids who have been through divorce will end up smarter about what it takes to create a successful relationship. Perhaps you will be more careful about who you'll marry and will avoid making some of the same mistakes your parents made. Now that would be great!

Your Turn _____

How do you feel about relationships and marriage?

Do you wonder whether most marriages can't work?

Are you scared of getting hurt if you get involved? What have you learned from your parents' divorce that you would bring into a relationship when you get older?

One thing I've learned about what it takes to have a good marriage is _____
_____
_____
_____.

• • • • • • • • • • • • • • • •

I'M A DIFFERENT PERSON THAN MY PARENTS. MY LIFE WILL BE DIFFERENT THAN THEIRS.

• • • • • • • • • • • • • • • •

If You Blame One of Your Parents for the Divorce

19

COPING WITH BEING ANGRY AT YOUR MOM OR DAD

Zoe: Some kids are really mad at one of their parents because they think the divorce was all their fault. For example, the parent is an alcoholic or was abusive or had an affair or wouldn't get marriage counseling. You have a right to be angry, because they've hurt you and your family and their behavior has caused your life to turn upside down.

Evan: You're right, that it's okay to be angry. But even though it's really hard, you also have to try to be forgiving. People aren't bad, they just sometimes do bad things. It may seem super, super hard, but your parents are your "creator" and you just need to go deep in your heart and find the love inside of you to forgive. Give yourself some time to do that. Don't expect to feel good about the parent you're mad at right away. These things take time. You can be mad at one of your parents, but don't block them out because they're still your parent.

Zoe: You need to remember that parents are just people—they do make mistakes. But you still get to be mad. It doesn't mean you're going to be angry at them for the rest of your life. If you can't tell your parent you're mad, tell somebody else. It might take until you're older 'til you can work this out. These things are more complicated than you think. It takes two to tango, so even though you're sure one of your parents is to blame, there's usually two sides to every story.

Dear Zoe,

I feel so sorry for my dad. My mom walked out on him and is getting married to someone else. My dad's a mess. He can't even go to work. I live with my mother and I just hate her for what's she's done to my dad. I'd live with him if I could, but for now, how do I handle my feelings toward my mom?

Brian, age 12

Dear Brian,

You're in a really tough situation. It's normal to be angry at your mom. And it's normal to want to help your dad, but you can't make his hurt go away or change the past. You can be extra nice to him and listen to his feelings, but he shouldn't criticize your mom to you even if she's hurt him really badly. Besides, you probably don't know the whole story, there may be more to it than you've been told. Don't assume that your mom's necessarily the only bad guy, she might have really good reasons for leaving your dad. You should talk to her and try to get more information, which might help you be a little more forgiving.

Sincerely,
Zoe

1. Write a letter to the parent you're mad at to try to get your feelings out.

2. Think about the times when you've made mistakes.

3. Let yourself be angry until you're done being angry.

4. If you can, try to let it go.

5. Get your anger out in other ways, like hitting a pillow or putting on loud music and singing or screaming at the top of your lungs.

What Their Mom Has to Say

Plenty of kids blame one of their parents for the divorce—and in plenty of cases, there's good reason to do so. For example, there are unfortunate situations in which a parent is abusive, has an affair, refuses to get help for a drinking or drug problem, or even just leaves because he or she can't handle the responsibilities of having a family.

When these sorts of things happen, it's perfectly appropriate to be angry and betrayed. If this describes one of your parents, you have every right to be angry, but there's still a good reason for trying to accept and forgive. Anger, even when it's for a good reason, hardens our heart and ends up making us feel bad inside.

While it may seem difficult—or even impossible—to forgive your parent, here's two things to remember: First, everyone makes mistakes—even grown-ups! Second, when people do bad things, it's usually because they're having problems that keep them from being their best selves. This doesn't excuse your parent's behavior, but it may make it easier to understand and forgive them.

There are also kids who are so angry and hurt, they blame their parents for the divorce even if neither their mom nor their dad did anything wrong. It may take time to forgive your parents for putting you through a divorce. But hopefully, in time, you will realize that the last thing they ever wanted to do was to hurt you. If they could have avoided this, believe me, they would have.

Your Turn _____

Do you blame either or both of your parents for the divorce? If so, why?

Write down the reasons why you may be angry at one or both of your parents. It doesn't matter whether or not your feelings are justified. They're still your feelings, and all feelings are real, whether or not they're based in reality.

Start by completing this sentence:

I'm angry at my mom or dad for _____

_____

_____.

Here's what I'd really like to say to my mom or dad: _____

_____

_____.

I could forgive him or her more easily if _____

_____

_____.

· · · · · · · · · · · · · · · · · ·

EVERYONE MAKES MISTAKES.

· · · · · · · · · · · · · · · · · ·

Rewards, or the Good Things No One Tells You about Divorce 20

Evan: It's so dumb that everyone acts like divorce is the end of the world. There are so many good things that come out of it. Going through this has made me emotionally tougher. When you go through something hard, you get stronger. The whole thing has made me more durable and more sympathetic. I mean, I'd never experienced agony before. Now I know how it feels when your heart breaks; it's a huge dark feeling that surrounds you and there's no way to escape.

Zoe: I felt that way, too. But now I feel older and wiser because of what I've been through. I know about different kinds of families and I'm more accepting when something bad happens, because I am confident I'll survive. When my friends have problems with their families, they come to me because I've been through it. Divorce may seem like the worst thing that could happen, but you have this tragedy and you find out that you can endure.

Evan: One thing I like about it is that I have more time and attention from each of my parents. When they were married, I got 50 percent of each of them. Now, I get almost 75 percent because they're only concentrating on me when we're together.

Zoe: There are lots of plusses to being divorced. You get two houses, more parents, more life experiences that make you a better person.

I've had to learn how to deal with problems, like accepting my father being gay, like dealing with attitude from kids at school who don't get it, like having to be more organized and not always getting to be with the parent I want to when I want to.

Evan: I like spending separate time with Mom and Dad, because both of them are a lot happier now. Lots of families stay together for their children's sake and have terrible lives. Our family is doing great. My parents are happy and I'm happy. I still have my old friends and I've made new friends because my parents are divorced—we have something in common. I like both of my parents' new partners and I like both places I live. So everything's turned out fine. If you come into this situation with a made-up mind that's it's going to be awful and you're not going to learn anything, then you won't. It's a given that it's going to be hard, but that doesn't make it bad. This is the sort of thing you have to find out for yourself.

Dear Zoe,

I get sick of people feeling sorry for me because my parents got divorced. Some of my friends say, "Oh, that must be so hard for you," or grown-ups keep asking how I'm doing and I don't know what to say. Sometimes I'm sad that my parents aren't together anymore, but I've adjusted, and to tell you the truth, I feel pretty good about the situation. I don't have to listen to them argue anymore, and they're both being really understanding and nice about what I need. Why do people have to act like you're some kind of a freak or have an incurable illness just because your parents are divorced?

Janet, age 13

Dear Janet,

People say things like that because they don't understand. They think you're in a terrible crisis, but they don't know the first thing about it if they've never been through it themselves. Yes, they're trying to help, but they shouldn't feel sympathetic because divorce isn't a bad thing. It's just something that happens which usually turns out for the best. The next time someone acts this way, just be quick and sassy about it. Say "I'm happy and I'm fine." If you know that you're okay and strong, then you can just flow with it and not feel as if you have to defend yourself to anyone.

Best of luck,
Zoe

Evan's Quick Tips

1. Think about the good things you've gotten out of divorce.

2. Know that your parents are probably happier apart.

3. Remember the bad stuff that went on when they were married.

4. Realize how you're growing from going through this.

5. See how much your life has improved.

What Their Mom Has to Say

It's a shame that people think that divorce is only a horrible thing. In fact, I can think of dozens of ways in which going through my divorce has changed my life for the better and has made Zoe and Evan far stronger and more capable human beings. But I certainly didn't know this when their dad and I first told them we were getting divorced. Back then, I was terribly worried that our divorce would ruin their lives, that they would feel troubled and insecure, and that perhaps they would be rejected by their friends. Boy, was I wrong!

Writing this book has convinced me that divorce can have a positive impact on kids. I've seen how Zoe and Evan, like so many other kids, are stronger and more resilient from having been through this. Those of you who go through divorce are not only survivors—you are heroes! You have so much to be proud of. You're more flexible because you've had to get used to so many new things, like two homes, stepparents, and the countless other ways your life has changed. You're more responsible because you've learned how to organize your schedules and your belongings.

But most of all, you've learned a lot about love. Like Zoe and Evan, going through divorce has probably made you more caring and compassionate, more able to lend a hand when your friends are hurting or in need. You know what it's like to feel sad, and you know how to listen from your heart when others are in pain. And hopefully, you've learned that divorce isn't the end of the world. In fact, it can be a wonderful new beginning.

Your Turn _____

Can you see some ways in which your life has changed for the better as a result of your parents getting divorced?

How are you different? Stronger? More capable?

What have you learned?

Take a moment now to complete this sentence:

Since my parents got divorced, I can see how I've changed for the better by becoming more _____

_____

_____.

. . . .

I HAVE LEARNED A LOT AND
I WILL KEEP LEARNING AND
GROWING FROM THIS EXPERI-
ENCE.

. . . .